HOW TO CLOSE YOUR BUSINESS LEGALLY AND *GRACEFULLY*

Your Easy Step-by-Step Guide to Closing a Business

Made Simple

Dr. Rosie Milligan

Published And Distributed By
Professional Publishing House LLC
1425 W. Manchester Ave. Ste B
Los Angeles, California 90047
323-750-3592
Email: professionalpublishinghouse@yahoo.com
www.Professionalpublishinghouse.com

Cover design: TWA Solutions
First printing June 2024
978-1-7328982-7-1
10987654321

Disclaimer:

This step-by-step guide is designed to help you close your business smoothly, minimizing the risk of severe personal financial consequences. While the information provided is comprehensive, it does not replace the need for professional legal counsel.

I strongly urge you to engage a qualified attorney to address any legal intricacies pertinent to your business closure and consult a certified tax accountant for tailored tax advice specific to your situation.

Though I am not a certified attorney or tax professional, my decades of firsthand experience as the owner of several successful businesses, a seasoned senior estate planner, business consultant, and business coach have equipped me with the knowledge to guide you. I have led numerous thriving ventures and assisted countless individuals in navigating the complexities of entrepreneurship. This guide offers insights and strategies to empower your entrepreneurial journey, ensuring a smooth and secure transition as you close your business.

Acknowledgments, Dedications, and Thanks
From Dr. Rosie Milligan

First and foremost, I want to thank my late father, Simon Hunter, a Mississippi farmer whose legacy extends far beyond his work in the fields. As an entrepreneur who owned his farm, he introduced me to the world of business at the age of thirteen. I vividly remember selling watermelons from his patch, learning the basics of "Marketing 101." When I asked my father, "How do you know how much to plant each year?" He replied, "I know how much my children will eat, and I know how much the neighbors will steal." This wisdom has shaped my business expectations— always striving to get the most out of every opportunity.

I also want to express my deepest gratitude to my dear sister and best friend, Attorney Clara King. Her insights into the legal aspects of business have been invaluable, and she trained me to become one of Los Angeles's top estate planners.

This book is dedicated to every entrepreneur, regardless of the level of success you have achieved. Your determination to carve out your own path is commendable, and I applaud your courage and perseverance.

I dedicate this book to my youngest son and business sidekick, Cedric Andrea Milligan, Sr. Your unwavering support during our travels and dedication to maintaining the business in my absence is invaluable. Your inspiration ignited my passion for educating aspiring entrepreneurs about the benefits of choosing the LLC business entity. Thank you for being my rock and driving force on this incredible journey.

A heartfelt thank you to my children: Pamela Milligan-McGee, M.D., John Sherman Milligan, Jr., and Cedric Andrea Milligan, Sr. Your unwavering encouragement and support has been invaluable. Your cooperation allowed me to travel the country for lectures and book signings with peace of mind, knowing you were taking care of everything at home. This book is as much a testament to your support as it is to my efforts.

About Dr. Rosie Milligan

Dr. Rosie Milligan, a woman who knows no limits, is a prominent figure in the business and financial world, known for her multifaceted roles and exceptional expertise. As the CEO of Professional Business Management & Consulting Services and the Founder of My Tech Academy, she has established herself as one of Los Angeles's renowned financial gurus. Her extensive background includes being a seasoned senior estate planner, business coach, business consultant, and holder of a Ph.D. in Business Administration. Her motto: "Erase 'NO,' Step Over 'CAN'T,' and Move Forward With Life" has been a motivating influence for hundreds to whom she has been a mentor and role model.

Dr. Milligan's reputation extends nationwide, with individuals and organizations seeking her out for top-tier business and financial coaching services. With over twenty-six authored books and four hundred fifty books published for other authors, she owns the largest and most prominent

African American publishing house in the nation. In addition, she hosts a talk show that further solidifies her influence and reach.

Dr. Milligan's approach revolves around imparting expert guidance to bid farewell to mediocrity. Leveraging her impressive educational achievements, a wealth of business experiences, and years spent consulting non-profit organizations, startups, and established businesses, she offers membership packages that incorporate her personalized coaching methods and proven, effective business strategies. This combination has consistently produced tangible results, ensuring a pathway to a thriving business.

Want to learn more about Dr. Rosie?
Visit her websites:
www.drrosie.com
www.mytechacademy.net.

TABLE OF CONTENTS

INTRODUCTION

S tarting a business requires careful planning, extensive research, and a deep understanding of legal and financial responsibilities. Equally important, however, is having the proper knowledge about how to close your business. Just as there are legal ramifications when starting your business, there are also significant legal considerations when you decide to close your business.

Closing a business involves much more than simply making the decision, notifying your landlord, moving your equipment, and placing a "closed" sign on your door. There are numerous closure steps you must take to comply with city, state, and federal regulations. Failing to address these steps properly can leave you entangled in various financial liabilities, such as debts to the IRS, state and local governments, and State Franchise Boards.

Consider this scenario: A client in California closed her LLC business but did not notify the State Franchise Board of her business dissolution. Two years later, she received a substantial tax bill from the State Franchise Board, which included fees for failure to file, penalty fees, and the $800 annual filing fee required for operating an LLC in California. Unable to pay these fees, she eventually received a notice of levy. She could have avoided this situation entirely if she had properly dissolved her business and notified the appropriate authorities.

Each state has different laws and regulations regarding opening and dissolving various types of business entities. It is crucial to check the specific requirements for the state in which you operate your business. You can find much of this information on the websites of relevant government organizations.

When you decide to close your business, it is advisable to consult with legal and tax professionals to ensure you are following the correct procedures. Properly closing your business does not exempt you from tax obligations, but it helps you avoid unnecessary penalties and financial burdens.

In this book, *How to Close Your Business Legally and Gracefully*, I will guide you through the essential steps to closing your business properly. From notifying stakeholders and settling financial obligations to canceling registrations and filing final tax returns, this comprehensive guide will ensure you navigate the closure process smoothly and in full compliance with the law.

CHAPTER 1
How To Close An LLC Business

Dissolving a Limited Liability Company (LLC) involves several steps, which can vary depending on the state in which you registered the LLC. However, there are common steps that most LLCs will follow:

1. **Member Approval**:

   Obtain agreement from all members of the LLC to dissolve the company. This may require a formal vote or written consent, depending on the operating agreement.

2. **Review Governing Documents and State Laws**:

   Check the LLC's operating agreement and state laws to ensure compliance with any specific procedures or requirements for dissolution.

3. **File Articles of Dissolution**:

Submit the necessary dissolution forms (often called "Articles of Dissolution" or "Certificate of Dissolution") to the state's Secretary of State or equivalent agency. There is usually a fee for filing these forms.

4. **Notify Creditors and Settle Debts**:

Inform all creditors and settle any outstanding debts or obligations. This step might involve sending a formal notice to creditors and paying off any liabilities.

5. **Liquidate Assets**:

Sell off the LLC's assets and distribute the proceeds to the members according to their ownership interests and any agreements in place.

6. **File Final Tax Returns**:

File the final federal, state, and local tax returns, and pay any remaining taxes. Inform the IRS and state tax authorities that you are dissolving the LLC.

7. **Cancel Permits, Licenses, and Business Names**:

Cancel any business permits or licenses associated with the LLC and withdraw any business name registrations.

8. **Maintain Records**:

Keep detailed records of the dissolution process and any final transactions for a specified period as required by law.

Detailed Steps

1. **Member Approval**:

Hold a meeting if required and record the decision in the meeting minutes or through a written consent form.

2. **Articles of Dissolution**:

Obtain the appropriate form from the state's business filing office. Complete and submit it, along with the required fee. For example, in California, file this form with the Secretary of State.

3. **Notify Creditors**:

Prepare a letter to notify all creditors of the LLC's dissolution and provide them with instructions for submitting claims.

4. **Liquidate Assets**:

Sell the LLC's assets and convert them to cash. If there are physical assets, this might involve holding a sale or auction.

5. **Distribute Remaining Assets**:

   After paying off debts, distribute any remaining assets to members in accordance with the operating agreement or state law.

6. **File Final Tax Returns**:

   Close the LLC's Employer Identification Number (EIN) account with the IRS if applicable. File final state and federal tax returns and pay any outstanding taxes.

7. **Cancel Registrations**:

   Cancel business licenses, permits, and any registered trade names or DBAs.

8. **Record Keeping**:

   Store all documents related to the dissolution, including minutes of meetings, consent forms, tax returns, and notices to creditors.

Example Process for California:

1. **Member Approval**: Obtain consent from all members as per the operating agreement.

2. **Articles of Dissolution**: File Form LLC-3 (Certificate of Dissolution) and Form LLC-4/7 (Certificate of Cancellation).

3. **Notify Creditors**: Send written notices to creditors.

4. **Liquidate Assets**: Sell assets and settle debts.

5. **Distribute Assets**: Follow the operating agreement for distributing remaining assets.

6. **Final Tax Returns**: File final tax returns and pay all taxes.

7. **Cancel Registrations**: Cancel any business permits and the LLC's EIN with the IRS.

8. **Maintain Records**: Keep all dissolution documents for future reference.

Always consult with a legal professional or accountant to ensure that you've properly addressed all legal and financial obligations.

CHAPTER 2
How to Close an S Corporation

Dissolving an S Corporation involves several steps, which can vary depending on the state in which you registered the corporation. Below are the general steps required.

Steps to Dissolve an S Corporation

1. **Shareholder Approval:**
   Obtain approval from the shareholders to dissolve the corporation. This typically requires a vote and adherence to the procedures outlined in the corporation's bylaws.

2. **File Articles of Dissolution**:
   File the necessary dissolution forms, often called "Articles of Dissolution" or "Certificate of Dissolution," with the state's Secretary of State or equivalent agency. There is usually a fee for this filing.

3. **Notify Creditors and Settle Debts:**
   Inform all creditors of the dissolution and settle any outstanding debts and obligations. This might involve sending formal notices to creditors.

4. **Liquidate Assets:**
   Sell the corporation's assets and distribute the proceeds to pay off debts. You should distribute any remaining assets to shareholders according to their ownership percentages.

5. **File Final Tax Returns:**
   File the final federal, state, and local tax returns, and pay any remaining taxes. Inform the IRS and state tax authorities that you are dissolving the corporation.

6. **Cancel Permits, Licenses, and Business Names:**
   Cancel any business permits or licenses associated with the corporation and withdraw any business name registrations.

7. **Maintain Records:**
   Keep detailed records of the dissolution process and any final transactions for a specified period as required by law.

Detailed Steps

1. **Shareholder Approval:**
   Hold a formal meeting to vote on the dissolution. Ensure the decision is recorded in the meeting minutes or through a written consent form, adhering to the corporation's bylaws and state laws.

2. **File Articles of Dissolution:**
   Obtain the necessary form from the state's business filing office. Complete and submit it, along with the required fee. For example, in California, you would file Form DISS STK (Certificate of Dissolution) and Form DISS NP (Certificate of Election to Wind Up and Dissolve) if applicable.

3. **Notify Creditors:**
   Prepare and send a letter to notify all creditors of the corporation's dissolution. Provide instructions for submitting claims and ensure to settle all debts.

4. **Liquidate Assets:**
   Convert the corporation's assets into cash by selling them. If there are physical assets, this might involve holding a sale or auction. Use the proceeds to pay off any remaining debts.

5. **Distribute Remaining Assets:**

   After settling debts, distribute any remaining assets to shareholders in accordance with their ownership interests and the corporation's bylaws.

6. **File Final Tax Returns:**

   File the final federal, state, and local tax returns, including IRS Form 1120S (U.S. Income Tax Return for an S Corporation). Pay any remaining taxes and inform the IRS of the dissolution. You may need to check the box, indicating that it is the final return.

7. **Cancel Registrations:**

   Cancel business licenses, permits, and any registered trade names or DBAs. Close the corporation's Employer Identification Number (EIN) account with the IRS, if applicable.

8. **Record Keeping:**

   Maintain all documents related to the dissolution, such as minutes of meetings, consent forms, tax returns, and notices to creditors, for a period specified by state law or best practices (usually several years).

Example Process for California:

1. **Shareholder Approval:** Hold a meeting, vote on dissolution, and record the decision in the minutes.

2. **Articles of Dissolution:** File Form DISS STK with the California Secretary of State.

3. **Notify Creditors**: Send written notices to creditors and settle any debts.

4. **Liquidate Assets**: Sell assets and use proceeds to pay off debts

5. **Distribute Assets:** Distribute any remaining assets to shareholders as per their ownership interests.

6. **Final Tax Returns:** File final tax returns with the IRS and the California Franchise Tax Board, paying any remaining taxes.

7. **Cancel Registrations:** Cancel business permits and close the corporation's EIN with the IRS.

8. **Maintain Records:** Keep all dissolution-related documents for future reference.

Always consult with a legal professional or accountant to ensure that you properly address all legal and financial obligations and navigate any specific state requirements.

CHAPTER 3

How to Close a C Corporation

Closing a C Corporation involves several steps to ensure that you properly handle all legal and financial obligations. Here's a comprehensive guide to closing a C Corporation:

1. Board Approval and Shareholder Vote

    Board Resolution: The board of directors must meet to propose the dissolution of the corporation. You must document this proposal in a board resolution.

    Shareholder Approval: Shareholders must vote on the resolution. The approval typically requires a majority vote, but the exact requirement can vary based on the corporation's bylaws.

2. File Articles of Dissolution

    Prepare and File: Draft and file an Articles of Dissolution with the state in which you incorporated the corporation. The specific form and filing requirements vary by state.

Pay Fees: There may be filing fees associated with the dissolution process.

3. Notify the IRS and Close Accounts

Form 966: File Form 966, Corporate Dissolution or Liquidation, with the IRS within 30 days of the resolution to dissolve.

Final Tax Return: File the corporation's final tax return. Indicate that it is the final return on the form.

Cancel EIN: Write a letter to the IRS to cancel the corporation's Employer Identification Number (EIN) and close the IRS business account.

4. Settle Debts and Obligations

Notify Creditors: Inform creditors and settle any outstanding debts. This may include publishing a notice of dissolution in a local newspaper if required by state law.

Terminate Contracts: Cancel leases, contracts, and other agreements the corporation has entered into.

5. Distribute Remaining Assets

Inventory Assets: List all remaining corporate assets.

Pay Final Expenses: Use the remaining assets to pay any final expenses, including taxes, salaries, and legal fees.

Distribute to Shareholders: Distribute any remaining assets to shareholders according to their ownership percentage after you've settled all liabilities.

6. Comply with State Requirements

State Filings: Complete any additional state-required filings, such as a final annual report.

Business Licenses: Cancel any state or local business licenses and permits.

7. Maintain Records

Retain Documents: Keep the corporation's records for a specified period as required by state law and for tax purposes. This includes tax returns, dissolution documents, and records of asset distributions.

Additional Considerations

Legal Advice: Consult with an attorney to ensure compliance with all legal requirements.

Tax Advice: Seek advice from a tax professional to manage any tax implications related to the dissolution.

By following these steps, you can systematically close a C Corporation while meeting all legal and financial obligations.

CHAPTER 4

How to Close a Partnership Buisness

Closing a partnership business involves several steps to ensure you properly handle all legal, financial, and operational aspects. Here's a comprehensive guide:

1. **Review the Partnership Agreement**

   Check Dissolution Terms: Review the partnership agreement for any specific terms or conditions regarding the dissolution process. Unanimous Decision:

   Ensure all partners agree to dissolve the partnership, as required by the agreement.

1. **Vote on Dissolution**

   Formal Meeting: Hold a meeting with all partners to vote on the dissolution.

   Document the Decision: Record the decision in meeting minutes or a formal dissolution agreement signed by all partners.

1. **Notify Stakeholders**

   Employees: Inform employees about the closure and provide details on final paychecks, benefits, and any assistance with finding new employment.

   Customers and Clients: Notify customers and clients about the business closure and how it will impact them.

   Creditors and Lenders: Inform creditors and lenders, and arrange to pay off any outstanding debts.

2. **Settle Financial Obligations**

   Accounts Receivable: Collect any outstanding accounts receivable.

   Accounts Payable: Pay off all outstanding bills and debts.

   Tax Obligations: File final tax returns and settle any remaining tax liabilities.

3. **Distribute Remaining Assets**

   Liquidate Assets: Sell the partnership's assets if necessary to pay off debts.

   Distribute to Partners: Distribute any remaining assets to the partners according to the partnership agreement.

4. **Cancel Registrations and Permits**

   Business Licenses and Permits: Cancel any business licenses, permits, and registrations with local, state, and federal authorities.

   Trade Names: Cancel any registered trade names or DBAs (Doing Business As).

5. **File Dissolution Forms**

   State Government: File a dissolution form with the state where you registered the partnership.

   IRS: Notify the IRS of the business closure and file any necessary forms.

6. **Maintain Records**

   Financial Records: Keep copies of all financial records, tax filings, and dissolution documents for a specified period as required by law.

7. **Legal Considerations**

   Legal Counsel: Consult with an attorney to ensure you have properly addressed all legal aspects of the dissolution and to avoid future liabilities.

Example Checklist for Closing a Partnership Business

1. Review Partnership Agreement
2. Vote on Dissolution

3. Notify Employees
4. Notify Customers and Clients
5. Notify Creditors and Lenders
6. Collect Accounts Receivable
7. Pay Accounts Payable
8. Settle Tax Obligations
9. Liquidate Assets
10. Distribute Remaining Assets
11. Cancel Business Licenses and Permits
12. File Dissolution Forms with the State
13. Notify the IRS
14. Maintain Records

Closing a partnership business involves careful planning and execution to ensure you have met all obligations and the process is smooth. It's advisable to work with legal and financial professionals to navigate the complexities of the dissolution process.

CHAPTER 5

How to Close a Limited Partnership

Closing a limited partnership (LP) involves several legal and procedural steps to ensure that you've met all obligations and you complete the process correctly. Here's a detailed guide:

1. **Review Partnership Agreement**

    Check for Dissolution Provisions: The partnership agreement often outlines the procedure for dissolution. Follow these provisions carefully.

    Approval for Dissolution: Typically, the decision to dissolve must be agreed upon by the partners as specified in the partnership agreement.

2. **Vote to Dissolve**

    Partner Meeting: Hold a meeting of the partners to vote on the dissolution. Document this decision in the meeting minutes.

3. File Certificate of Dissolution

Prepare and File: Draft and file a Certificate of Dissolution (or similar document) with the state where you registered your LP. This form can usually be obtained from the state's business filing office.

Filing Fees: Pay any required filing fees.

4. Notify the IRS and Close Accounts

Final Tax Return: File the partnership's final tax return and mark it as final.

Cancel EIN: Send a letter to the IRS to cancel the Employer Identification Number (EIN) and close the IRS business account.

Notify Tax Authorities: Inform state and local tax authorities of the dissolution.

5. Notify Creditors and Settle Debts

Creditor Notification: Notify all creditors of the dissolution and settle any outstanding debts. This may include publishing a notice of dissolution in a local newspaper if required by state law.

Terminate Contracts: Cancel any ongoing contracts or leases.

6. Liquidate and Distribute Assets

Inventory Assets: Create a list of the partnership's assets.

Pay Final Expenses: Use the partnership's assets to pay off any remaining expenses, including taxes and debts.

Distribute Remaining Assets: Distribute any remaining assets to the partners according to their ownership interests, as specified in the partnership agreement.

7. Cancel Registrations, Permits, and Licenses

State Filings: Complete any additional required state filings, such as a final annual report.

Business Licenses: Cancel any business licenses, permits, and registrations obtained in the name of the partnership.

8. Maintain Records

Retain Documents: Keep all relevant records, including dissolution documents, final tax returns, and records of asset distributions, for a period specified by state law and for tax purposes.

Additional Considerations

Legal Advice: Consult with an attorney to ensure that all legal requirements are met and to navigate any complexities in the dissolution process.

Tax Advice: Seek advice from a tax professional to manage any tax implications related to the dissolution.

By following these steps, you can ensure that the dissolution of your limited partnership is handled thoroughly and in compliance with all legal and financial obligations.

CHAPTER 6

How to Close a General Partnership Business

Closing a general partnership involves several steps to ensure that you properly address all legal, financial, and administrative responsibilities. Here's a comprehensive guide:

1. **Review the Partnership Agreement**

   Check Dissolution Provisions: Review the partnership agreement for any specific procedures or requirements for dissolution. Follow these provisions carefully.

   Unanimous Consent: Typically, all partners must agree to dissolve the partnership unless the agreement specifies otherwise.

2. **Vote to Dissolve**

   Formal Decision: Hold a meeting with all partners to discuss and vote on the dissolution of the partnership. Document the decision in meeting minutes or a dissolution agreement.

3. File a Dissolution Notice

State Filing: File a Certificate of Dissolution or similar document with the state where you registered the partnership. This form can usually be obtained from the state's business filing office.

Pay Filing Fees: Pay any required filing fees.

4. Notify the IRS and Close Accounts

Final Tax Return: File the partnership's final tax return (Form 1065 in the U.S.) and mark it as the final return.

Cancel EIN: Send a letter to the IRS requesting the cancellation of the Employer Identification Number (EIN) and closure of the IRS business account.

Notify State and Local Tax Authorities: Inform state and local tax authorities of the dissolution and settle any outstanding tax obligations.

5. Settle Debts and Obligations

Creditor Notification: Inform all creditors of the dissolution and settle any outstanding debts. This may include publishing a notice of dissolution in a local newspaper if required by state law.

Terminate Contracts: Cancel any leases, contracts, and other agreements that the partnership is a party to.

Employee Notification: Inform employees of the closure and handle final paychecks, accrued benefits, and required tax filings.

6. **Liquidate Partnership Assets**

Inventory Assets: Make a comprehensive list of all partnership assets.

Sell or Distribute Assets: Sell off partnership assets or distribute them to the partners according to their ownership interests and the terms of the partnership agreement.

Settle Final Expenses: Use the proceeds from the asset sale to pay off any remaining expenses, including taxes and legal fees.

7. **Distribute Remaining Assets**

Asset Distribution: Distribute any remaining assets to the partners according to their ownership percentages, as specified in the partnership agreement.

Obtain Receipts: Have partners sign receipts for any distributions received, documenting that they have received their share.

8. **Cancel Registrations, Licenses, and Permits**

Business Licenses: Cancel any business licenses, permits, and registrations with state, local, and federal agencies.

9. Maintain Records

Retain Documents: Keep all relevant records, including dissolution documents, final tax returns, and records of asset distributions, for a specified period as required by law (typically 3-7 years).

10. Notify Stakeholders

Clients and Customers: Inform clients, customers, and other stakeholders of the partnership's closure. Provide instructions for any pending matters.

Public Announcement: If appropriate, make a public announcement or issue a press release about the dissolution.

Additional Considerations

Legal Advice: Consult with an attorney to ensure you've met all legal requirements and navigate any complexities in the dissolution process.

Tax Advice: Seek advice from a tax professional to manage any tax implications related to the dissolution.

By following these steps, you can systematically close a general partnership while ensuring compliance with all legal and financial obligations.

CHAPTER 7

How to Close a Sole Proprietorship Business

Closing a sole proprietorship involves several important steps to ensure that all legal, financial, and operational matters are properly handled. Here's a detailed guide to help you through the process:

1. **Decide to Close Your Business**

   Reflect and Plan: Make a definitive decision to close your business. Assess your reasons and ensure this is the best course of action.

2. **Notify Stakeholders**

   Employees: Inform any employees about the closure. Provide information on final paychecks, benefits, and any severance packages.

   Customers and Clients: Notify customers and clients about your decision to close. Complete any outstanding orders or contracts and communicate how the closure will affect them.

Suppliers and Vendors: Inform your suppliers and vendors. Settle any outstanding invoices and discuss the return of any unsold inventory or materials.

3. Settle Financial Obligations

Collect Accounts Receivable: Ensure all outstanding invoices are collected before closing.

Pay Off Debts: Settle any outstanding debts and liabilities with creditors and lenders.

4. Cancel Registrations, Permits, and Licenses

Business Licenses and Permits: Cancel any business licenses, permits, and registrations with local, state, and federal authorities.

Trade Names: Cancel any registered trade names or DBAs (Doing Business As).

5. Handle Final Tax Obligations

Final Tax Returns: File your final income tax return, indicating that it is the final return for your business.

Employment Taxes: If you had employees, make final federal and state employment tax deposits and file the final employment tax returns.

6. Close Business Accounts

Bank Accounts: After you've settled all financial transactions, close your business bank accounts.

Dr. Rosie Milligan

Credit Accounts: Close any business credit accounts.

7. **Notify the IRS and State Tax Authorities**

Federal Tax Forms: Notify the IRS by filing a final Schedule C with your federal income tax return.

State Tax Forms: File any required final state tax returns and pay any state taxes due.

8. **Maintain Records**

Financial Records: Keep copies of all financial records, tax filings, and dissolution documents for a specified period as required by law, typically for at least seven years.

Employee Records: Maintain records related to employees, such as payroll and employment tax records, for at least four years.

9. **Consult Professionals**

Legal Counsel: Consult with an attorney to ensure you've properly addressed all legal aspects of closing your business to avoid future liabilities.

Financial Advisor: Work with a financial advisor to ensure you've met all financial obligations and to help with the final accounting.

40

Example Checklist for Closing a Sole Proprietorship

1. Decide to Close Your Business
2. Notify Employees
3. Notify Customers and Clients
4. Notify Suppliers and Vendors
5. Collect Accounts Receivable
6. Pay Off Debts
7. Cancel Business Licenses and Permits
8. Cancel Trade Names
9. File Final Tax Returns
10. Make Final Employment Tax Deposits and Filings
11. Close Business Bank Accounts
12. Close Business Credit Accounts
13. Notify the IRS
14. Notify State Tax Authorities
15. Maintain Financial and Employee Records
16. Consult Legal Counsel
17. Consult Financial Advisor

Closing a sole proprietorship involves meticulous attention to detail and a thorough execution of several steps. By following this guide, you can ensure that your business is closed properly, fulfilling all legal and financial obligations. Working with professionals like attorneys and financial advisors can help you navigate the complexities of the closure process smoothly.

CHAPTER 8

How to Close a Non-Profit Organization Business

Closing a non-profit organization involves a series of legal, financial, and administrative steps to ensure compliance with federal and state laws. Here's a comprehensive guide to help you navigate the process:

1. Board Approval

Board Resolution: The board of directors must meet to approve the dissolution. Document the decision with a formal resolution.

Vote: Ensure that the dissolution is approved according to the organization's bylaws, typically requiring a majority vote.

2. Review Governing Documents

Bylaws and Articles: Review the organization's bylaws and articles of incorporation for any specific procedures or requirements related to dissolution.

3. Notify the State

File Articles of Dissolution: File Articles of Dissolution with the state where the non-profit is incorporated. This form can usually be obtained from the state's business filing office.

Filing Fees: Pay any required filing fees.

4. Notify the IRS

Final Tax Return: File the final federal tax return (Form 990 series) and indicate that it is the final return.

Termination Notice: Submit a letter to the IRS to notify them of the dissolution, including a copy of the Articles of Dissolution.

Form 990: Depending on the size and type of the non-profit, file the appropriate version of Form 990 (990, 990-EZ, 990-N).

5. Settle Debts and Obligations

Notify Creditors: Inform all creditors of the dissolution and settle any outstanding debts.

Terminate Contracts: Cancel any leases, contracts, and other agreements.

Employee Notification: Inform employees of the closure and handle final paychecks, accrued benefits, and required tax filings.

6. Distribute Remaining Assets

Asset Distribution: Distribute the non-profit's remaining assets according to state laws and the organization's bylaws. Typically, assets must be transferred to another tax-exempt organization.

Document Transfers: Keep detailed records of how and to whom the assets were distributed.

7. Cancel Registrations, Licenses, and Permits

State and Local Authorities: Cancel any business licenses, permits, and registrations.

Charitable Solicitation Registration: Notify the state's charity regulator (often the Attorney General) of the dissolution.

8. Maintain Records

Retain Documents: Keep all relevant records, including dissolution documents, tax filings, and records of asset distributions, for a specified period as required by law (typically 3-7 years).

9. Notify Stakeholders

Donors and Members: Inform donors, members, and other key stakeholders of the organization's closure.

Public Announcement: If appropriate, make a public announcement or issue a press release about the closure.

Additional Considerations

Legal Advice: Consulting with an attorney experienced in non-profit law can help ensure all legal requirements are met.

Tax Advice: A tax professional can assist with managing tax implications and ensuring all necessary filings are completed correctly.

By following these steps, you can ensure that the dissolution of your non-profit organization is handled thoroughly and in compliance with all legal and financial obligations.

CONCLUSION

No entrepreneur sets out with the intention of closing their business. However, unforeseen circumstances can sometimes force this difficult decision. Many entrepreneurs find themselves in business by default, lacking formal training or prior experience. The post COVID-19 era has exacerbated this, pushing many to pursue self-employment out of necessity.

As a business consultant and coach, I have seen numerous entrepreneurs face significant tax liabilities due to improper business closures and failing to notify the relevant city, state, and federal agencies. This book addresses that gap, offering clear, comprehensive guidance on how to close a business correctly—a topic often overlooked in the vast literature on starting and managing businesses.

The steps to close a business can be complex and vary depending on the business type and location. This book provides the essential steps to help you navigate this process legally and gracefully. My hope is that you find success in your business endeavors and never need to close your business. But if that time comes, this book will be your guide to doing it right.

For further insights into business, I recommend reading my other books: "What You Need to Know Before You Start A Business" and "LLC & S Corporation Essentials: Your Ultimate FAQ Guide for Entrepreneurs Made Simple." You can order them from Amazon.com, Barnes & Noble. com, ProfessionalPublishingHouse.com, and DrRosie.com.

Thank you for entrusting me with your journey. Remember, whether you are starting or closing a business, having the right knowledge and tools is crucial.

www.ingramcontent.com/pod-product-compliance
Lightning Source LLC
Chambersburg PA
CBHW032020190326
41520CB00007B/553